Amazing
Animal Camouflage

by Alix Wood

WINDMILL
BOOKS ™

New York

Published in 2013 by Windmill Books,
An Imprint of Rosen Publishing
29 East 21st Street, New York, NY 10010

Editor for Alix Wood Books: Mark Sachner
US Editor: Sara Antill
Designer: Alix Wood
Consultant: Sally Morgan

Photo Credits: Cover, 1, 2, 3, 4, 5, 6, 7, 8, 9 (top), 10, 11 (top), 12, 13, 14, 15, 16, 17, 18, 19, 20, 21, 22, 23 © Shutterstock; 9 (bottom) © Photo Resource Hawaii/Alamy; 11 (bottom) © Amy D. Moore; 13 (bottom) © Kris H. Light; 17 (top) © Getty Images; 18 (top) © Stephen Childs

Library of Congress Cataloging-in-Publication Data

Wood, Alix.
 Amazing animal camouflage / by Alix Wood.
    p. cm. — (Wow! wildlife)
 Includes index.
 ISBN 978-1-4488-8097-3 (library binding) — ISBN 978-1-4488-8166-6 (pbk.) —
ISBN 978-1-4488-8168-0 (6-pack)
 1. Camouflage (Biology)—Juvenile literature. I. Title.
 QL759.W656 2013
 591.47'2—dc23

                        2011051690

Manufactured in the United States of America

CPSIA Compliance Information: Batch #B1S12WM: For Further Information contact Windmill Books, New York, New York at 1-866-478-0556

Contents

What Is Camouflage?

Life in the wild can be dangerous. One of the most amazing ways a creature can make sure it survives is by using **camouflage**. Camouflage means using colors or patterns to blend with the surroundings. Some animals pretend to be plants, ground cover, or even other animals, in order to hide or to hunt.

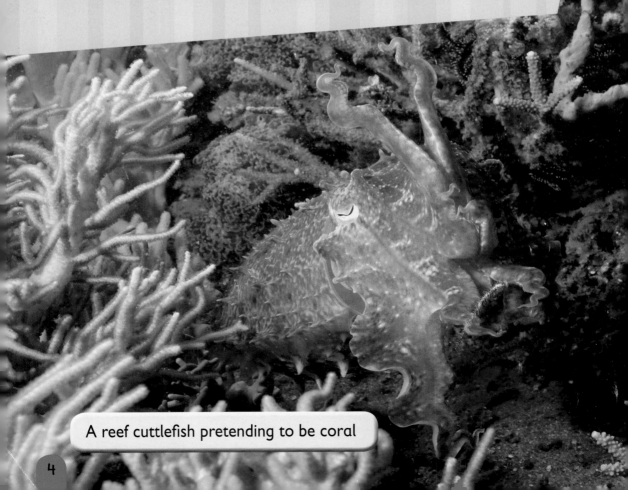

A reef cuttlefish pretending to be coral

Can you spot the difference between these two butterflies? No? Neither can birds. The one on the top is a harmless Viceroy butterfly. It pretends to be the poisonous Monarch butterfly (on the bottom). Sometimes you don't have to blend in to not get eaten. Just pretend to be something you're not!

WOW! It's Not Good to Stand Out!

By matching its surroundings, an animal can often live longer. Babies will usually be the same color as their parents. So, over time, the animals develop the perfect colors for survival. Those with poor camouflage are easily hunted and are easily seen when they are hunting. They won't live long enough to have babies.

Which of these barking deer is easier to see in the forest?

5

Blending into the Background

Looking like its background helps an animal in two ways. First, it can hide from **predators**. Second, it can sneak up on its food. For example, forest animals are often brown to match tree trunks and soil.

This frog's skin is a perfect color for blending in with its background!

The underside of a frog is usually light. When seen from underwater, it gives the frog camouflage against the pale sky.

Who's Hiding in the Forest?

Young deer have white spots on their backs. The spots look like dappled sunlight on the forest floor. The spots disappear when the deer gets its first winter coat. This happens when it is about four months old.

Changing Colors

Some creatures change their color to match changes in the color of their environment. For example, this Arctic fox may *blend* in with its snowy **habitat** now. But what about when the snow melts?

When the snow melts, an amazing thing happens. The color of the fox's coat changes to match its habitat! The fox loses its white coat and grows a new coat that is a different color.

An Arctic fox in spring

Chameleons are amazing color-changers. Did you know that they change their color when their mood changes, not when they move to different surroundings?

A young panther chameleon

WOW! You Are What You Eat!

This cute Hawaiian happy-face spider changes color depending on what it eats! It is usually a see-through yellow color, but it changes to orange if it eats flies, moths, or butterflies. It turns green if it eats caterpillars and **aphids**.

Patterns

Many animals have unusual designs on their bodies. Spots and stripes help animals match their surroundings. Patterns can blur an animal's outline. It is hard for **prey** or predators to see where the animal begins and ends.

Animals in jungles or tall grass may have long, **vertical** stripes. This Bengal tiger lives in the jungle. Its vertical stripes help it blend in among the trees.

Leopards stalk their prey until they are so close they can almost touch them. They need good camouflage to sneak up so close!

When hunting, leopards hold their tails down so the white tip doesn't show.

A giant panda's black and white pattern makes it seem to disappear in the snowy mountains in winter. Even in summer, its outline is broken up and hard to see.

WOW! **Keep Still, Mom!**

Ruffed grouse nest on the ground. The camouflaged mother (above) sits on the nest all day to hide her white eggs (left). She only leaves to feed at dawn and dusk.

Safety in Numbers

Living in groups can keep animals safer. In a group, there are more eyes to spot both food and danger. Moving together as a large mass confuses predators, too.

Being nearly see-through is great camouflage against predators! Glassfish swim in large **schools**. From above, their dark backs blend in with the color of the sea. Seen from below, their pale undersides merge with the light from the sky.

The black and white colors of zebra stripes may not look like camouflage. The pattern is much more important than its color, though. The stripes blend in with tall grass. It doesn't matter that the zebra's stripes are black and white, because the zebra's main predator, the lion, is thought to be **color-blind**!

A zebra herd looks like one large, moving, striped mass. The herd confuses lions. They have trouble picking out any one zebra.

One zebra's stripes blend in with the stripes of the zebras around it.

WOW! Fake Snake

When tiny fungus gnats hatch, they cling together and move like a big snake. That must scare off hungry birds!

Underwater Masters of Disguise

Some of the most clever camouflage is underwater. Creatures make themselves look like plants, stones, or the sandy floor. This sort of camouflage doesn't hide the animal. It disguises it to look like something else!

Leafy seadragons have flowing flaps of skin that look just like pieces of seaweed.

When a hippo hides halfway underwater, it looks just like a large boulder! The hippo's eyes, nose, and ears are on the top of its head. It can hide in the water and *still* be able to see, hear, and breathe!

WOW! A Deadly Stone

The stonefish is the most **venomous** fish in the world. Almost invisible on the ocean floor, it has needle-like spines that stick up when it is threatened.

A flounder disguised as the sandy seabed

Look Like a Stick!

Some creatures **mimic** leaves, sticks, or tree bark to keep from being eaten. Many of these mimics are insects. The predators they are trying to fool are often birds.

This stick insect is also called a walking stick. If it keeps still, it is very hard to spot. It can also sway when it moves, like a stick blowing in the wind!

Bird Droppings Caterpillar

An Asian swallowtail butterfly caterpillar

This weird caterpillar disguises itself as bird waste to keep from being eaten! When it gets too large to pass for bird droppings, it turns a bright leaf-green color!

The leaf katydid is a great mimic. Some types even have spots and rough edges on their wings. These look like the dried edges of a leaf that is dying.

Clever Fur and Skin

Animals can use the **texture** of their fur or skin to help them blend in with their environment. So a squirrel's rough, uneven coat isn't there by accident! The texture helps it blend in with the bark of a tree.

These two photos are both of a mimic octopus. It can change its appearance by tightening or loosening muscles in its skin. Doing this can change its texture and color. Sometimes it even buries some of its arms to fool you!

WOW! Countershading

Some animals, like this squirrel (above) and otter (right), are dark on top and light underneath. This is called **countershading**. It makes the animal look flat as the lighter fur evens out the shadow made by daylight. It is hard to see the squirrel from a distance. In water, the otter's white belly makes it harder to see against the sunlight when fish are looking up at it.

Looking Dangerous or Delicious

Many harmless animals mimic more harmful creatures to scare off predators. Some animals lure their prey by looking like a wiggly worm! Others look just like their prey, so they can sneak up on them in plain sight.

The back of the hawk moth caterpillar (left) looks like a snake head. This is a scary sight for predators!

WOW! My Scary Eyes

When frightened, the automeris moth opens its wings to show its scary eyespots. Fake eyes fool enemies away from its real head, so the moth may survive an attack.

WOW! An Ant? Count the Legs...

The ant mimic spider makes itself look just like its ant prey. The spider has eight legs. This could spoil the surprise, but the spider lifts its two front legs to make them look like **antennae**!

The alligator snapping turtle has a worm-shaped wiggler on the tip of its tongue. The turtle lies very still in the water with its mouth wide open. The wiggly worm lures fish into the turtle's mouth. Then its powerful jaws snap shut!

The alligator snapping turtle is often camouflaged with **algae**.

Glossary

algae (plural of *alga*) (AL-jee)
Plantlike life forms that mostly grow in water.

antennae (an-TEH-nee)
Movable feelers on an insect's head.

aphids (AY-fidz)
Tiny soft-bodied insects that suck the juices of plants.

camouflage (KA-muh-flahj)
The hiding or disguising of something by covering it up or changing the way it looks.

color-blind (KUH-lur-blynd)
Being partly or totally unable to tell the difference between one or more colors.

countershading (KOWN-tur-shayd-ing)
Camouflage that is dark on top and light underneath.

habitat (HA-buh-tat)
The place or type of place where a plant or animal naturally or normally lives or grows.

mimic (MIH-mik)
To look like something else.

predators (PREH-duh-terz)
Animals that live by killing
and eating other animals.

prey (PRAY)
An animal hunted or killed
by another animal for food.

schools (SKOOLZ)
Large numbers of fish swimming
together.

venomous (VEH-nuh-mis)
Having or producing poison.

texture (TEKS-chur)
The structure, feel, and look
of something.

vertical (VER-tih-kul)
Going straight up or down from
a level surface.

Websites

For web resources related to the
subject of this book, go to:
www.windmillbooks.com/weblinks
and select this book's title.

Read More

Racanelli, Maria. *Camouflaged Creatures*. Crazy Nature. New York: PowerKids Press, 2010.

Underwood, Deborah. *Hiding in Forests*. Creature Camouflage. Chicago: Heinemann-Raintree, 2010.

Weber, Belinda. *Animal Disguises*. Science Kids. New York: Kingfisher, 2007.

Index